gift K
to Scot.

Oktoberfest
2007

MW01341644

There is a proverb that is thousands of years old
and speaks of peace and prosperity in the city:

● ● ● ● ●

'THUS SAYS THE LORD OF HOSTS,
"OLD MEN AND OLD WOMEN WILL AGAIN SIT IN THE STREETS,
AND EACH MAN WITH HIS STAFF IN HIS HAND BECAUSE OF AGE.
AND THE STREETS OF THE CITY WILL BE FILLED WITH BOYS AND GIRLS

PLAYING IN ITS STREETS."'

Zechariah 8: 5 New American Standard Bible

Picture Perfect Waxahachie
The best town in Texas!!

Produced by Great Collections Publications of Waxahachie, Texas

Book Publisher & Designer: Kevin Haislip

Principle Contributing Photographers:
Lynn Cromer,
Kevin Haislip,
Sally Owens,
Ami Trull

Forward by Wanda Cain, pages 5, 6
Introduction by Kevin Haislip, pages 7, 8
'It's the People' by Neal White, pages 27, 28
'Sidewalk Museum' by Robert Lynn, pages 49, 50
'Larger than Life' by Debra Wakeland, pages 66-70
'I Love Waxahachie' by Mayor Joe Jenkins, pages 87, 88
'Epilogue' by Kevin Haislip, publisher, page 123

Copyright © 2007 by Kevin Haislip, Great Collections Publications
All rights reserved. No part of this book may be used, or reproduced in any manner whatsoever without the written permission of the Publisher.
Printed in the United States of America.

Picture Perfect Waxahachie, The best town in Texas!!
ISBN: 978-0-9795010-0-5

Cover photograph of Courthouse by Lynn Cromer,
Cover Design by Kevin Haislip.
Back cover photograph of earth courtesy of NASA.

PICTURE PERFECT

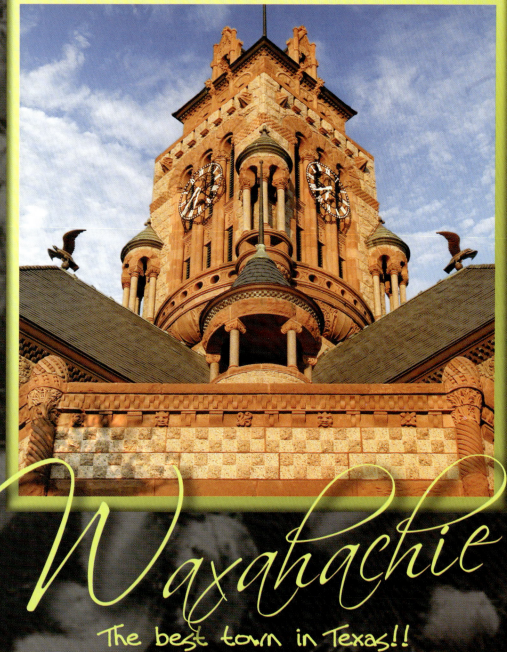

Waxahachie
The best town in Texas!!

Publisher: Kevin Haislip
Sponsors: Citizen's National Bank of Texas, Waxahachie Downtown Merchants Association
and Convention & Visitors Bureau, The Waxahachie Daily Light
Contributing Photographers and Writers: Lynn Cromer, Kevin Haislip, Sally Owens, Ami Trull
Wanda Cain, Mayor Joe Jenkins, Robert Lynn, Debra Wakeland, Neal White

Acknowledgements & Sponsors

Citizens National Bank of Texas
Your bank since 1868.

Waxahachie Downtown Merchants Association
and The Convention and Visitors Bureau

The Waxahachie Daily Light
Ellis County news and information
delivered fresh daily
since 1867.

Our thanks:

Those of us who have worked on this book have a profound debt of gratitude to many for their help and support. These friends are Holly Davis at the Ellis County Courthouse who was always quick to lend her influence and help when we needed it. John Smith at the City of Waxahachie who often mobilized help for our strange requests. Jody Haislip, Wanda Cain, Bonney Ramsey, and Sheryl Sullivan who proofed the pages of this book. If mistakes are found, it is because I failed to get them in place, and not because they missed anything with their sharp eyes. Bob Lynn, Debra Wakeland, and Laurie McPike Mosley who always seemed to know just the right person to talk to and opened doors that I didn't know existed. Andy Moya who gave some type suggestions. Several performed double duty such as our writers, Mayor Joe Jenkins, Neal White, Bob Lynn, Debra Wakeland, and Wanda Cain. And most importantly, our spouses and families who put up with the long late hours and the associated sacrifices. We thank you all very much for your help and contributions.
KRH

Dedicated to

the fine people of Waxahachie,
to everyone mentioned in these pages and those
we could not include because of room. We have something rare
here not often found in other communities and it takes a lot of tireless work
and love to make it all happen. Not content to rely on those who have gone
before us, we honor our heritage and take the lessons learned from
them and continue to build on what we were given. May we never
take it for granted and always be a grateful people.

Principle Contributing Photographers

Lynn Cromer Architectural Photography (214) 668-2857
Lynn is a Christian, husband, father and grandfather.
He finds the art of architectural photography a rewarding form of expression,
and is currently accepting a limited number of assignments.
He can also be reached at his email: txcromer@prodigy.net

Kevin Haislip, HaisliPhotography (972) 800-0307 Waxahachie 27 years
Portraits, Senior Portraits, Weddings: Treasures and heirlooms you will love.
Corporate and Industrial photography: Imaging solutions
for the Corporate Environment. Executive and Environmental Portraiture,
Industrial processes, Dramatic Product shots, for collateral brochures, Annual
Reports, and Advertising/Marketing.

Sally Owens, Something-to-Say Photography (469) 337-6099
"Founded in Waxahachie, Texas 2000 -
due entirely to the people of this community. I love
what you have given me to do! I thank you."

Ami Trull (214) 212-0723
Ivey Photography, Midlothian-TX
Portraits, Weddings, Families, Seniors
"Capturing the Art of Your Life"

Forward by Wanda Cain

Welcome to our beloved Waxahachie—the unique city of romance, history, and beauty. We proudly call ourselves "the best town in Texas" and you will surely agree after a tour of these pages.

Our unique name, Waxahachie, is but a foreshadowing of the richness of our city and its personality. Why was our town given such a hard-to-spell name? Perhaps it came from the Indians who found buffalo watering here on the creek and called the place "Waxahachie," meaning "cow" or "buffalo creek." But more romantic is the little-known tale that our city was named before a location was found. The tale claims some "powers that be" in Austin decreed that the county seat would be named "Waxahachie" wherever the city might be located.

Wherever we've traveled, we've met folks that know about Waxahachie. We met a woman traveling in New York who hailed from Australia. To our amazement, when we told her where we were from, she confided that she was born in Waxahachie to a Baptist minister and his wife! In England, we were signing a register in a museum and an on-looker asked us to pronounce our city's name. We did, and a British woman echoed from across the room, "We know where that is!" But there are those who say they moved to Ennis or Italy or other cities because they couldn't spell Waxahachie!

Everyone knows where Waxahachie is! The name is so rare that the world takes notice! The Zsohars, refugees from Hungary, tell the story of their relatives who sent them a letter from Hungary with the address simply "Dr. Zsohar, Waxahachie." Yes, they eventually got the letter!

Waxahachie is a city of memories and history. Many of us have been a part of our city for many years. For example, my first pair of shoes, now bronzed and on display in our home, came from Brooks Red Goose Shoe Store. My birth certificate, my first driver's license, and my marriage license were recorded here in the ever-growing files of our glorious courthouse that can tell tales of all the citizens—past and present.

We are a romantic people in all of our diverse backgrounds, interests, and talents. People of rare abilities come from

Photograph by Kevin Haislip

Photograph by Lynn Cromer

Photograph by Ami Trull

our city — artists, writers, musicians, movie stars, sports heroes, leaders in all walks of life. The city's unique personality can be seen in the names of streets and buildings that carry a proud tradition of family and history.

We glory in our beautiful city with its picturesque buildings and collections of tales from the past. Not only are we considered the "cotton queen" of the past, but we are also known as a city of romantic Victorian homes, many of which have historical markers. We are people who dream dreams and work to make them come true in education, art, architecture, churches, community, and in whatever we imagine.

We welcome with open arms and warm hospitality all who come here. We share our beauty with those who visit us whether they are just sight seeing, sharing our Bethlehem Revisited, touring the Gingerbread Trail, or enjoying one of our many holiday tours and parades.

Through the pages of this book we share our city with you in picture and dialogue, but only through a visit can you experience the beauty of our city and the warmth of our people.

Wanda Cain

Introduction
by Kevin Haislip

The first thing you notice as you drive down West Main Street into Waxahachie are the tree-lined lanes and the beautifully restored Victorian homes. From there, the enchantment only grows. On any given day, you might well find yourself in the middle of a parade, music festival, or crowds of people milling around the town square. It's a lot like walking onto the set of the *Music Man*, and you catch yourself looking over your shoulder expecting Harold Hill to be marching down the street with his band close behind.

It's the kind of town where people still sit on their front porches and greet neighbors as they walk past. Children play in the streets, and church steeples rise up on most corners pointing to God. On major holidays, the local Rotary club puts out American flags along the boulevards, and the cafes fill up as friends gather together for a meal, a few stories and jokes, and a good time.

Waxahachie has changed a lot in the last few years and is poised to change a lot more in the years to come. Today, it is a little older than 155 years and boasts a population of slightly over 28,000. About six to seven people a day move into this idyllic town, and houses are being built at a rate never before seen. They come because of its close proximity to Dallas and Fort Worth. But they make Waxahachie their home because of the charm and rich heritage.

This book is a testament to the people, the architecture, and all that makes our town what it is. The contributing photographers who took up this project did so with one thought in mind: to boast about our town. We had a very difficult time choosing what to focus our cameras on. We did the best we could. There was so much to show.

Photograph by Lynn Cromer

Photograph by Kevin Haislip

The Gingerbread Trail tour of historic homes in the summer, the Crape Myrtle Festival in early July, the Texas Country Reporter Festival in the fall, Bethlehem Revisited at Christmas and all the other festivals and celebrations make Waxahachie spectacular. There is always something fun and downhome friendly going on. Friendlier people can't be found anywhere.

See for yourself what we mean when we say, 'Picture Perfect Waxahachie.' It is the best town in Texas! And that my friend, is no brag.
It's fact!

Kevin Haislip, publisher

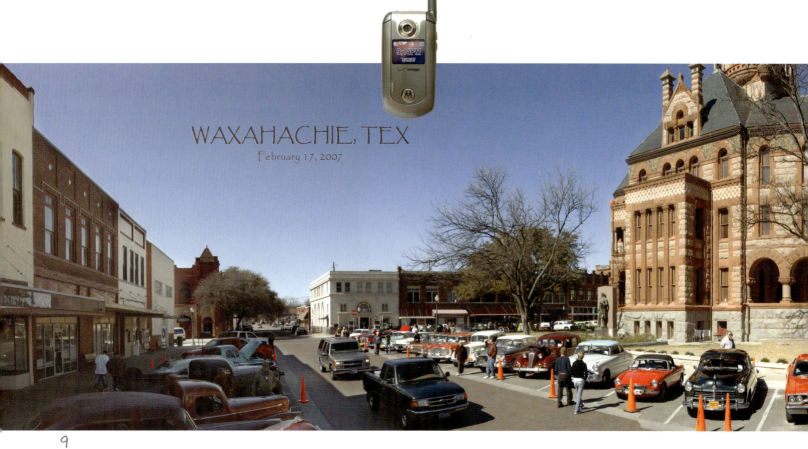

9

A wonderful day for a blast from the past Sweethearts and Orphans model cars on display around the Ellis County Courthouse. Proceeds benefit the American Heart Association.   Photograph by Kevin Haislip

Photograph by Lynn Cromer

Keith Roberts climbs out on the catwalks of the courthouse clocktower for ongoing maintenance and repair of the clock mechanisms. During the renovation of the courthouse in 1998, it was discovered the clanger had worn a significant dent in the bell from a century of ringing. So the bell was rotated around to another spot for the next 100 years. Photograph by Kevin Haislip

Photographer's Notes:
Monday, October 9, 2006, 1PM. Photographed the city of Waxahachie from the top ledge of the Waxahachie Courthouse. The ledge is all of eight inches wide, although it does have a stone wall that surrounds it.

Not surprisingly, about the only ones who ever get up here are the birds. For us humans to get to the ledge, we have to climb a 20 foot narrow circular stairwell, and then climb a vertical ladder another 25 feet past the clock faces to where the clock mechanism is kept. There are no nets to catch you if you fall.

The views from the clock tower are arranged with the northern view in the top center; southern view in the bottom center; eastern view in the right center; and western view in the left center. If you compare the square photographs shown here with photographs taken in 1919, not a lot has changed dramatically downtown. But the growth on the horizon, while covered by trees, is very different.

Photographs by Kevin Haislip

Photograph by Lynn Cromer

Second floor courtroom of the Ellis County Courthouse. Photograph by Lynn Cromer

Joe Suehlak opens the gate at the North Watertower on 287. Photograph by Kevin Haislip

Photograph by Lynn Cromer

Photograph by Ami Trull

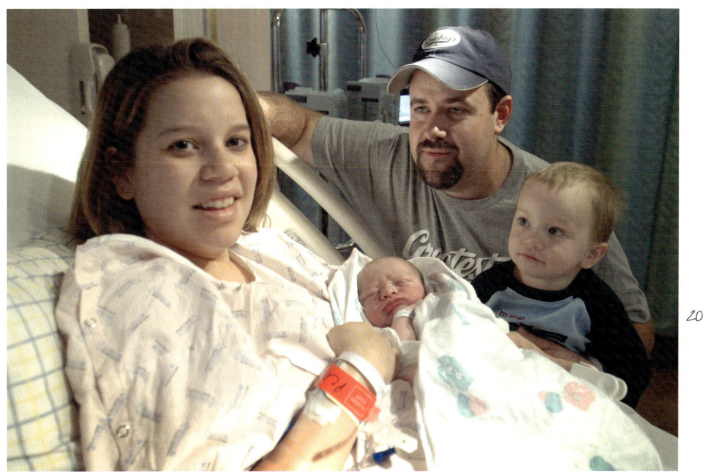

The birth of Hayden Goolsby at 7:36 in the morning of January 12, 2007 to Erika and Shane Goolsby at Baylor Medical Center at Waxahachie. He joins his brother Kolten. Photograph by Kevin Haislip

Barry Wolverton (l) and Ken Roberts (r) laugh it up at the KBEC morning Flea Market. The Flea Market has been on the air every day since September 1961, taking calls from listeners selling pianos and whatever else they have lying around. It is the proverbial backyard fence everyone gathers around for a bit of chit-chat and birthday wishes. Photograph by Kevin Haislip

Horace Bratcher is everywhere and knows everyone. He is as good as they get for sweet hometown people. Born in Waxahachie in 1926, he joined the Navy working on fighter planes before finishing Waxahachie High School. He became a barber in 1947, trained horses for 40 years, and worked in the school systen until retirement. He became an official member of the College Street Church of Christ in 1939, was a member of the Masons for 50 years, and the Odd Fellows for 60 years. Photograph by Ami Trull

Citizens National Bank of Texas... a pioneer in making people's dreams come true for more than 139 years.

Photograph by Kevin Haislip

A carriage ride through the park is a perfect way to spend an afternoon for Peggy Spalding and her friend. Photograph by Kevin Haislip

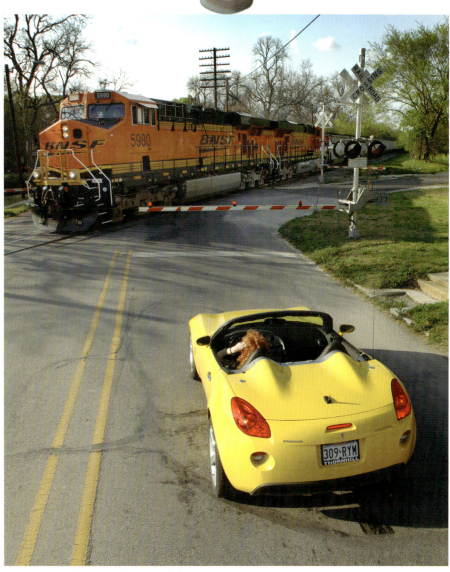

The comedic punchline of this photograph is not the sassy red head in her yellow sports car waiting on the train. It is what it took to get this photograph. On any given day, if you need to go across Waxahachie, you're likely going to be delayed by the train crossing. But for this re-creation, it took more than a dozen times parking by the RR crossing waiting for the train that seemed to never come.
Photograph by Kevin Haislip

It's the people
by Neal White

They are the heart and soul of our city. The way they interact in words and deeds is more telling of where we live than the noble and majestic structures that line our streets. In Waxahachie, it is the people who bring this city to life.

You don't have be in our city long to figure that out. When we pass on the street, we still wave to each other, with all of our fingers I might add. Men still tip their hat to a lady, and we still open doors for each other. We not only talk to our neighbors, we look out for each other. When someone is in need, everyone springs into action. I couldn't even begin to count how many of such stories I've worked on for the newspaper. Good news stories of neighbors helping neighbors, of families and businesses volunteering their time and dollars to help someone in need.

By modern standards, that might sound a little old fashioned, but that's what makes Waxahachie 'home.' In our town, you're not just a number on the population sign posted at the entrance to the city. In our town, you're expected to be an active participant. Here, each person is still valued for bringing a unique voice and his or her own set of God-given talents to the table. We are engaging. Come to think of it, we're pretty hospitable, too. Regardless of the occasion, there always seems to be room for one more at the table.

That's not to say that we always agree. We don't. But that's OK, because we're not afraid to bring our challenges to light, even though there are times when it gets a little uncomfortable. We face issues head-on, build consensus and together, work out ways to resolve them. I like to think it's the kind of community our forefathers had in mind when they set out to forge a new nation, a community filled with caring, compassionate people grateful for God's many blessings.

In Waxahachie, our most cherished blessing is our children. We're pretty proud of them, not just the ones that live under our roof, but all of them.

Photograph by Neal White

Photograph by Neal White

Photographs by Neal White

Far lower left: Martin Luther King Rally in the Courthouse square on Martin Luther King Jr.'s birthday.

Left two photos: Five year old Johnny Dineen was killed in a farming accident. The community and friends came to help the family finish their hay harvest.

Right photo: Graduation at Waxahachie High 2006.

The African proverb tells us that it takes a village to raise a child. The people of Waxahachie put those words into action every day. Through school and sports and extra curricular activities, bonds are formed and our families become extended. 'Like one of my own' is another expression that's pretty common in Waxahachie. It's often used when referring to a child you helped mentor in some way or another. In that sense of community, extended families quickly grow large in Waxahachie. The more you get involved in the community, the more lives you touch, and in turn, touch you.

It's the people.

In this quaint, charming town that stands out as an oasis in the midst of the encroaching urban sprawl of the Metroplex, Waxahachie is a place where people still matter. Although times are changing, it's still a place where folks prefer a face-to-face visit over a text message or e-mail. After all, it's hard to shake hands in cyberspace. In Waxahachie, you'd be amazed at how many problems are solved over a cup of coffee and little sage counsel. Maybe it's wishful thinking, but I'm convinced if we could bring Congress to Waxahachie for a day and have a sit down over a slice of pie from the 1879 Chisholm Grill, we'd see some real progress from lawmakers. In Waxahachie, we just find a way to make it happen.

Neal White is the publisher/editor of the Waxahachie Daily Light

Front porch sitting is a favorite with our wide verandas and neighborliness. Above, Tanya Jenkins enjoys a good book and the sunshine surrounded by the sweet smells of her garden. On the right, Marvin Silver catches up on the news.
Photographs by Kevin Haislip.

Michael Scudiero and Bobby Huskins enjoy the spring night air and some guitar picking. Photograph by Kevin Haislip

The day began with rain, but the sun came out in the afternoon in time for the wedding and all the celebrations for Alice Hadley and Joseph Lee Nichols.   Photograph by Kevin Haislip

Ed Mosemiller has been building cabinetry for homes, & doors like these at the Central Presbyterian Church on College Street since he was seven. Today, he is 86 years old, and still takes new projects in his shop on Water Street, on advise from his doctor, 'You have to remain active.' Photograph by Kevin Haislip

Only in Waxahachie would you see something like Ron Johnson out for a walk with his donkey.
Photograph by Kevin Haislip

Blake Howard & Amber Nealy out for a late summer Sunday evening jog down Grand Avenue.
Photograph by Kevin Haislip

Mike Hearron shows off one of his top selling watermelons at Farmers Market in the Courthouse square.
Photographs by Ami Trull

Bruce Zimmerman, Senior Pastor at Waxahachie Bible Church, preaches to the fire fighters on Sunday mornings before church services.   Photograph by Kevin Haislip

Above, Texas State Representative Jim Pitts in the gallery of the Texas State legislature in Austin. On the right, Rusty Ballard meets with US Congressman Joe Barton representing Ellis County. Photographs by Kevin Haislip

Joginder Bhore (Jo) immigrated to the United States in 1953 from Punjab, India. He came to Waxahachie in 1991 for the Superconducting Super Collider project as construction manager. When the project closed down, he and his family loved Waxahachie so much, they stayed. Though he has worked on major construction projects around the world, the one he favors the most was his role as Program Manager for the Ellis County Courthouse renovation in 1998.

Photograph by Kevin Haislip

Children's Mass at St. Joseph's Catholic Church. Photograph by Kevin Haislip

Waxahachie is a community of faith, and at Easter, families come to worship the risen Savior Jesus Christ at their church. This was at the United Methodist Church. Photographs by Kevin Haislip

Scarborough Renaissance Festival treats guests to a renaissance country faire with strolling characters, charming shoppes, and a Tournament field. Photographs provided courtesy of Scarborough Renaissance Festival

The Cow Creek Country Classic Bike Ride is Waxahachie Rotary Club's major fund raiser, attracting thousands of cyclists from all over. The funds raised have built a Boy Scout cabin in Chapman Park; contributed to new construction of a Boy's and Girl's Club at the Salvation Army facility; YMCA expansion projects; Baylor Medical Center at Waxahachie; and funded the start up of the first seven homesites for Ellis County Habitat for Humanity. Photograph by Kevin Haislip

Burvon King, a long-time Waxahachie resident, is the chairman of the deacon board at Greater Mt. Zion, and also tends the grounds of the church property. Photograph by Ami Trull

The ROMEOs (Retired Old Men Eating Out) have been meeting Saturday mornings for breakfast at the 1879 Chisholm Grill since 2004. Left to right: Calvin Nix, Jeff Gowesky, Terry Miller, Mike Downey, Les Collard, Lane Schumacher, Jack Wagner, Jon Gilliam, Richard Pace, Don Frisbee Jr., and Don Frisbee.
Photograph by Kevin Haislip

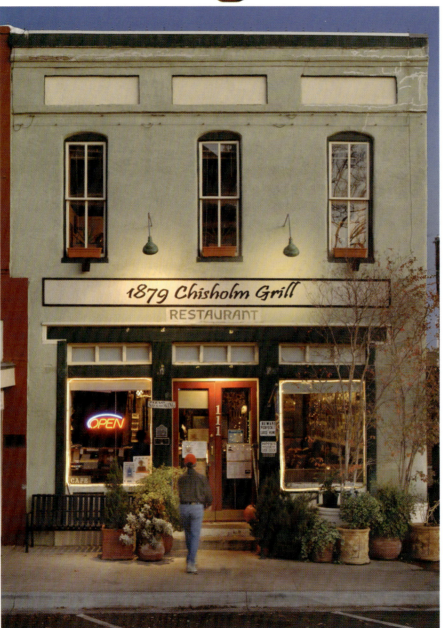

Don and Susan Simmons keep a pretty friendly place for all who come for a meal. Anyone who has been in town for more than 15 minutes has heard of the 1879 Chisholm Grill, and it won't be very long before old friendships are made. Photograph by Kevin Haislip

Photograph by Lynn Cromer

Photograph by Lynn Cromer

HISTORIC WAXAHACHIE INC.
RECOGNIZES THIS PROPERTY
BUILT C. 1900
AS WORTHY OF PRESERVATION

Photograph by Ami Trull

Waxahachie. The Sidewalk Museum. by Bob Lynn

Waxahachie is a Sidewalk Museum. Everywhere you turn there is a masterpiece hung on the horizon. And, as in any gallery of fine art, the closer you look at the overall canvas, the more you appreciate the refinements.

The pathways of the Sidewalk Museum are filled with color; Waxahachie is the Crape Myrtle Capital of Texas. Stately trees stand like museum sentries guarding aisles to the art. Lawns are manicured like polished green marble floors, and gardens cast out a wonderful scent of sweetness. Bread is baking, a player piano is tapping out ragtime, a new nest of chirpers is cradled in Gingerbread trim, you touch the mastery of 1800s craftsmanship, the sun caresses stained glass... every one of your senses is being touched along the corridors of the community.

Like any great museum, Waxahachie is not defined by any one piece of artwork. Many proclaim that the courthouse on the downtown square is the finest county seat building in all of Texas' 254 counties. Although that magnificent building may be an architectural anchor to the city, branching out in any direction is like going room-to-room in a great archive of art and seeing one masterpiece after another.

To understand the true beauty of Waxahachie you must take a quiet journey down its streets, stopping to experience and appreciate what the community has done to preserve history. The city is an archive of glorious, historic homes and buildings in tribute to a time gone by that has never left. Waxahachie is truly one of the world's most beautiful Sidewalk Museums.

Photograph by Kevin Haislip

Waxahachie Art Museum on Main Street.   Photograph by Lynn Cromer

51

LISTED IN THE
NATIONAL REGISTER
OF HISTORIC PLACES
BY THE UNITED STATES
DEPARTMENT OF THE INTERIOR

Photograph by Lynn Cromer

Photograph by Kevin Haislip

The Lyceum in the Nicholas P. Sims Library.   Photograph by Lynn Cromer

The Nicholas P. Sims Library on West Main Street.   Photograph by Lynn Cromer

55

Photograph by Lynn Cromer

HISTORIC WAXAHACHIE INC.
RECOGNIZES THIS PROPERTY
BUILT IN 1916
AS WORTHY OF PRESERVATION

Photograph by Lynn Cromer

WILLIAMS-ERWIN HOUSE
ERECTED IN 1893 FOR EDWARD WILLIAMS, THIS VICTORIAN HOME REFLECTS THE AFFLUENCE OF LOCAL COTTON MERCHANTS DURING THE LATE 19TH CENTURY. WAXAHACHIE CONTRACTOR C. J. GRIGGS SUPERVISED THE CONSTRUCTION. BEADED BOARDS AND SHINGLING DECORATE THE EXTERIOR WALLS, AND ELABORATE EASTLAKE STYLE DETAILING ADORNS THE PORCH. WILLIAMS SOLD THE HOUSE IN 1902 TO R. K. ERWIN, ANOTHER PROMINENT BUSINESSMAN. THE ERWIN FAMILY OWNED IT UNTIL 1943.
RECORDED TEXAS HISTORIC LANDMARK—1978

Photograph by Lynn Cromer

Photograph by Lynn Cromer

Southwestern Assemblies of God University (SAGU), Blake L. Farmer Administration Center (formerly Trinity University). Photograph by Lynn Cromer

HISTORIC WAXAHACHIE INC. RECOGNIZES THIS PROPERTY BUILT IN 1902 AS WORTHY OF PRESERVATION

Photograph by Lynn Cromer

Photograph by Lynn Cromer

HISTORIC WAXAHACHIE INC.
RECOGNIZES THIS PROPERTY
BUILT C. 1895
AS WORTHY OF PRESERVATION

Photograph by Lynn Cromer

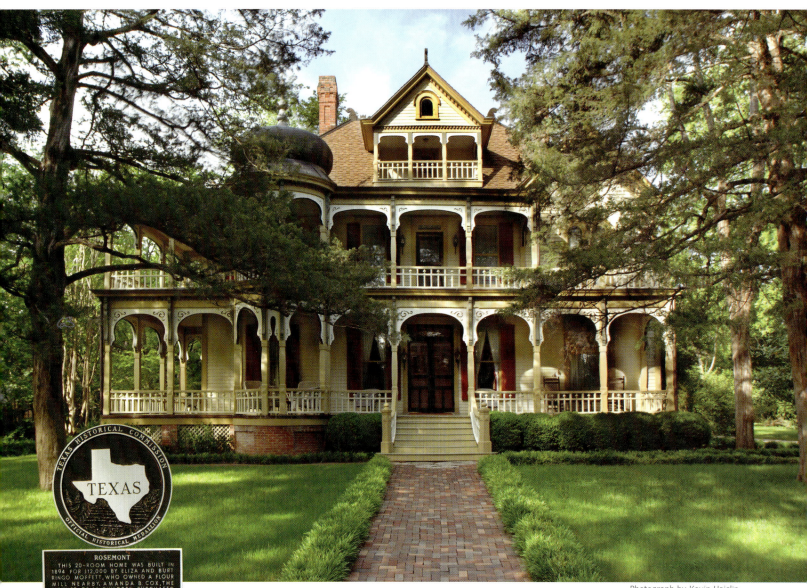

Photograph by Kevin Haislip

64

The Square is a favorite place for an evening stroll, a kiss and engagement portraits.
Photograph by Kevin Haislip

The Texas Music Theatre presents a wide variety of Texas music by the finest bands, singers, and songwriters on the Texas Music Scene. Last year 280+ shows were performed in the restored 1895 theatre. Photography by Ami Trull

Waxahachie Movie List

- Bonnie and Clyde, 1967 – Faye Dunaway, Warren Beatty, Gene Hackman, Estelle Parsons. Oscars for Best Supporting Actress (Parsons) and cinematography (Burnett Guffrey).
- Deadly Blessings, 1980 – Ernest Borgnine, Maren Jensen.
- Tender Mercies, 1981 – Robert Duvall, Tess Harper, Wilford Brimley. Oscars for Best Actor (Duvall) and Best Screenplay (Horton Foote).
- Of Mice and Men (TV), 1981 – Randy Quaid, Robert Blake.
- Cowboy (TV), 1981 – Ted Danson, James Brolin, Patrick Tovatt.
- Glory Road, 1982-83 – Gary Busey, Marjoe Gortner (film went bankrupt; never released).
- Ellie, 1983 – Pat Paulsen, Shelley Winters, George Gobel.
- Places in the Heart, 1983 – Sally Field, Danny Glover, John Malkovich, Ed Harris, Amy Madigan, Lindsay Crouse, Bert Remsen. Oscars for Best Actress (Field) and Best Screenplay (Waxahachie Native, Robert Benton).
- 1918, 1984 – Matthew Broderick.
- The Last of the Caddoes (TV)
- The Aurora Encounter, 1984 – Jack Elam.
- Peyton Place: The Next Generation, 1985 – Dorothy Malone, Ed Nelson.
- The Trip to Bountiful, 1985 – Geraldine Page, Rebecca DeMornay, John Heard, Carlin Glynn. Oscar for Best Actress (Page).
- Valentine's Day, 1985 – Matthew Broderick, William Converse Robert.
- True Stories, 1985 – David Byrne.
- Thompson's Last Run, 1985 – Robert Mitchum.
- The All-American Cowboy, (TV special) with Charlie Pride.
- Katherine Anne Porter: A Texas Childhood (TV), 1986.
- Square Dance, 1986 – Jason Robards, Jane Alexander, Winona Ryder, Rob Lowe.
- Traveling Man, 1987 – Kay Lenz.
- The Fig Tree, 1987-88 – William Converse Roberts, Theresa Wright, Doris Roberts.
- Norman Rockwells's Breaking Home Ties, 1987-88 – Jason Robards, Eva Marie Saint, Doug McKeon, Erin Gray, Claire Trevor.
- It Takes Two (working title: My New Car), 1987-88 – Patrick Dempsey, Leslie Hope Barry Corbin.
- River Bend (originally titled Night of the Eagles, and previously titled Give or Take a Hundred Years), filmed in 1987-88; released in 1989 – Steve James, Margaret Avery.
- Ollie Hopnoodle's Haven of Bliss, 1987-88 – James B. Sikking, Jean Shepherd.
- Born on the Fourth of July, 1987-88 – Tom Cruise (only one small scene in rural part of county).
- Love Hurts, 1987-88 – Jeff Daniels, Cloris Leachman.
- Bonnie & Clyde: The True Story, 1991.
- Pure Country, 1993 – George Strait.
- Curse of the Starving Class, 1994 – James Woods, Kathy Bates, Lou Gossett Jr., Randy Quaid, Henry Thomas.
- Universal Soldier: The Return, 1999 – Jean-Claude Van Damme.
- Walker, Texas Ranger (TV Series), 1993-2000.
- Slap Her . . . She's French, 2001 – Piper Perabo, Jane McGregor, Trent Ford.
- Fat Girls, 2005 – Ash Christian.
- Walking Tall 2, 2006 – Kevin Sorbo.
- Walking Tall 3, 2006 – Kevin Sorbo.
- Prison Break (TV Series), Season 2 - 2006.

Larger Than Life in Waxahachie
by Debra Wakeland

Waxahachie – from a film site standpoint – has been called 'The Best Little Hollywood in Texas' and 'vintage America in mint condition.' That's no brag, folks. Just the facts.

Waxahachie's Rise as a Filming Location: Back in the days when it was a hot spot for film shoots, wags used to call this county seat 'the back lot of Dallas.' Waxahachie's popularity as a location in the 1970s and 1980s grew out of the D/FW area's unique advantages as well as its own. As a national production center, Dallas/Fort Worth was one of the few areas outside of Los Angeles or New York offering film companies both the economies of production and available crews and resources they required. Less expensive location fees and other lower costs were also an additional attraction. Waxahachie was one of the closest communities to the Dallas crew base offering a small-town America look with an attractive square and period homes and buildings--for instance, the set for *1918* that surpassed anything Hollywood carpenters could build on a back lot.

Hollywood on the Prairie: Waxahachians like to call their city, the Hollywood of Texas--and not without good reason. The filmmaking began here with *Bonnie and Clyde*, scripted by Waxahachie native Robert Benton, which was filmed in the Dallas area in 1967. It reached its pinnacle in the early '80s when Benton returned to his former hometown to write and direct the Oscar-winning feature *Places in the Heart*, starring Sally Field. Two other Oscar-winners *Tender Mercies*, starring Robert Duvall and Tess Harper, and *The Trip to Bountiful* were shot principally in Waxahachie at that time. The average reader probably does not know that Jerry Haynes, best known to Dallas/Fort Worth and national audiences as 'Mr. Peppermint,' played the deputy sheriff in the 1983 feature film *Places in the Heart*. Waxahachie served as a perfect setting for period films, as well as for motion pictures that were seeking to capture the flavor, the aura, the mystique of small-town rural America. As *The Detroit News* said about Waxahachie: 'Quiet back streets are a trip back to the 1890s, when cotton was king. Horses still graze in the yards of Victorian mansions and little wooden cottages.' And *The New York Times* reported in 1987: "Waxahachie has a stately granite courthouse on the main square and enough 19th century homes with wide verandas, as front porches were called in better families, to organize an annual tour. It has a cemetery shaded by live oak trees that by now must be one of the most photographed graveyards in the country." Waxahachie was unique among area small cities in actively soliciting the movie industry. It was a seller's market for the city. Another advantage was that, because of the above movies, Waxahachie may have been the only quintessential small town in the area with which the state film commission was truly familiar. Among these additional Waxahachie projects were the Horton Foote scripted *1918* and *Square Dance*, starring Rob Lowe and Winona Ryder. The abandoned Superconducting Super Collider site did find new life when *Universal Soldier* came into town in 1999 and used the site for the film. *Curse of the Starving Class*, starring Kathy Bates and James

Writer/director/star Dolph Lundgren prepares for the next scene of his movie 'Missionary Man', on the site of the historic courthouse building in Waxahachie, Texas.
Copyright Sony Pictures. All Rights Reserved.
Photograph by Neil Jacobs/Sony Pictures

Woods, was set at the site of the Ellis County jail, thanks to working with past County Judge Penny Redington. The Chamber of Commerce and Convention & Visitors Bureau were involved in film to the point of developing an Ellis County Head Book & Property Reference Guide. It was a one-stop shop for filmmakers.

Mr. Waxahachie: In 1986, Waxahachie was hopping with film and media thanks to the late L.T. Felty, the city's biggest film booster, who was instrumental in winning locations for many films in the county, and who had the opportunity to assist in the casting of some of the films. He was Waxahachie's very own unofficial film commissioner and movie public relations man. He was also the Chili Advisor to the Governor. His tireless efforts continued to ensure work in the film industry until his death. The city owes much gratitude to Mr. L.T. Felty, who will hold the title forever as "Mr. Waxahachie."

Film Commission: Waxahachie was a founding member of the Film Commission of North Texas: In1987, through a task force led by Senator Kay Bailey Hutchison. The Dallas/Fort Worth Regional Film Commission, renamed, was an economic development/tourism promotion consortium, comprised of North Texas cities, chambers of commerce and convention & visitors bureaus (also supported by private sector members). The commission was instrumental in soliciting and coordinating film and video production for the D/FW area. Chuck Beatty and this writer represented the City of Waxahachie on this Board. We were heavily involved in the organization and were familiar with production needs, assisting film prospects on various projects, and often were available to guide scouts to desired locations.

The Gingerbread City and its World-Wide Acclaim as the Unrivaled Movie Capital of Texas: Cities compete for films due to the economic impact of the dollars spent locally, as well as for the impact on hotel and tourism industries. Applying standard economic impact multipliers, the total economic impact, for instance, of Sony Pictures' *Universal Soldier: The Return*, with Jean-Claude Van Damme, shot for four months at the former site of the Superconducting Super Collider, had an impact of as much as $15 million on the Waxahachie area. Total impact exceeded $50 million as those expenditures were recirculated in the local economy. *The Walker, Texas Ranger* series left approximately one million dollars per episode (or 50% of each episode's budget). In 1998, the industry's annual $90 million in direct expenditures and $300 million economic impact on North Texas gets one's attention. The City of Waxahachie recognizes motion picture and TV production as one of the best growth industries worthy of municipal investment.

Current Challenge for Waxahachie: There are now hundreds more municipalities and metropolitan areas competing for business than did in the early days when projects naturally gravitated to Dallas/Fort Worth. By the mid-'80s, most films were shot by independent production companies without union contracts, rather than by the major studios or networks who had to come here for union crews. Films now shoot elsewhere simply because they can; they have many more choices. Consequently, for most of the past decade, Austin has led the state in the amount of major motion picture production dollars attracted. It is true that Waxahachie has lost many productions that might once have come to this area, but are now directed to small Austin-Hill Country communities. Nevertheless, the quaint Hollywood of Texas does have local talent, a vibrant economy, cooperation of locals, right-to-work status (meaning lower cost on movies without higher union fees), good production facilities that are expanding, and the broadest array of landscapes a site manager could desire.

Waxahachie and Ellis County have been called Texas's welcome mat to visitors from the movie industry, and those welcome guests continue to show up at the door. In fact, it has been rumored that a Denzel Washington project has been scouting the Ellis County area. The Waxahachie Chamber of Commerce & CVB Director, Laurie McPike Mosley is said to be awaiting Denzel with open arms—with purely professional motivation, of course.

Debra Wakeland is the President & CEO of the Waxahachie Chamber of Commerce and Convention & Visitors Bureau where she has held this position since 2000. She was the Director of the Convention & Visitors Bureau from 1984 until 2000 whereby she worked with film request handling all media relations for the City of Waxahachie. She served on the North Texas Film Commission from 1986 until its demise.

Producer/director John Wilder (left) discusses a scene at the Waxahachie railroad depot with actor Jason Robards (center) and Doug McKeon for the Telecome Entertainment ABC movie of the week *Norman Rockwell's Breaking Home Ties,* which Mr. Wilder wrote based on a painting so titled by the artist. The period film shot in 1987 involved moving a 1950's era train to the station with the assistance of the Texas and D/FW Regional film commissions.

Jeff Daniels and Judith Ivey in a scene from the 1998 feature film *Love Hurts,* which used one of the many Waxahachie old Victorian homes as its principle location. Directed by Bud Yorkin, the comedy-drama also starred John Mahoney, Cynthia Sykes, Amy Wright, Cloris Leachman, and Thomas Allen.

Photograph by Sally Owens

A nearly exact replica of the Munster Mansion featured in the 1960's sitcom *The Munsters* is home to Charles and Sandra McKee. At Halloween, the couple opens their home to the public for tours to raise funds for various charities. Charles and Sandra host the event dressed as the very friendly and amicable Herman and Lily Munster. Photographs by Kevin Haislip

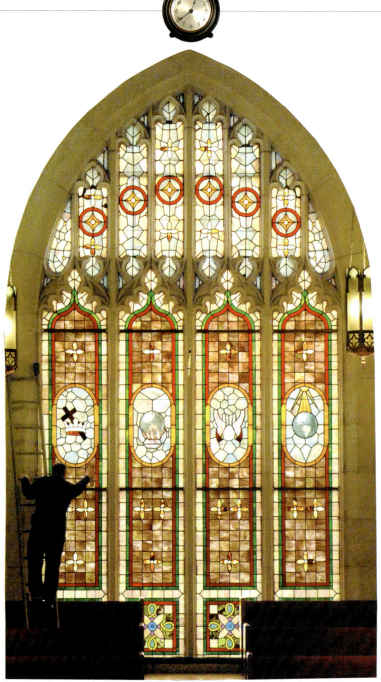

Last minute clean up follows three years of renovation of the First Baptist Church. Photograph by Kevin Haislip

That we never forget, 'The Price of Freedom' War Memorial is a vivid reminder to us of the brave men and women of Ellis County who have given that last measure to protect our freedoms. Photograph by Lynn Cromer

75

Always a big crowd pleaser, we love our high school sports.
Photographs by Ami Trull

Indians Varsity 2006. Photographs by Ami Trull

Photographs by Neal White

In the late summer and fall heat, the marching band can be seen every afternoon and evening practicing in the parking lot late. Their dedication and talent shows itself on the field.
Photographs by Ami Trull

Photograph by Ami Trull

Niqky Hughs triumphantly holds the 2006 District AAAA State Championship trophy for the Waxahachie High School Girls basketball team.
Photograph by Lezley Norris

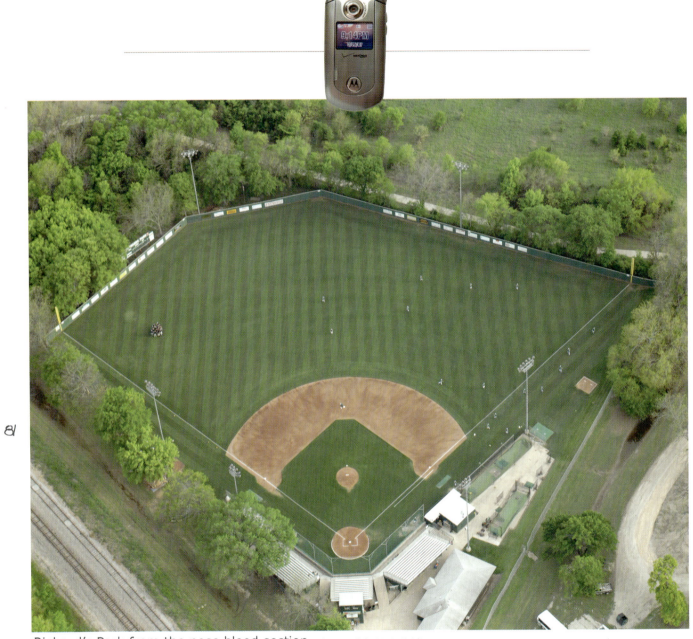

Richard's Park from the nose bleed section. Photograph by Kevin Haislip

It's the bottom of the ninth between the Washington Nationals and the Boston Red Sox, two Waxahachie Youth Baseball teams. The teams are 13 and 14 year old players. Photograph by Kevin Haislip

Texas Country Reporter Festival downtown on the square. Photograph by Kevin Haislip

The Crape Myrtle Queens (left to right), Judy Cross, Gladys Nay, Renda Hickerson, Shirly Singleton, Bonney Ramsey, Shirley Williams (current queen), and Susie Braden also known as 'Miz Myrtle'. In 1997, the Texas State Legislature recognized Waxahachie as the Crape Myrtle Capital of Texas. Since then, the Crape Myrtle Festival has been held every year on July 3rd and 4th with a concert, tailgate party, and fireworks. Photograph by Kevin Haislip

New homes are being constructed at a pace never before seen in Waxahachie and Ellis County with the population expected to triple in 25 years. Photograph by Kevin Haislip

Veterans Day WWII re-enactment of a battle with American and German forces draw soldiers and crowds.
Photograph by Kevin Haislip

Waxahachie! by Mayor Joe Jenkins

Yes, I love to talk about Waxahachie. Why is this? It's a feeling that quickly gets in the blood and and it doesn't take long. Let's take a look through my eyes to see our town.

I was born right here in Waxahachie, 1925 to be precise. I don't remember much about the Twenties, but the Thirties and Forties bring back wonderful warm memories in spite of the 'Great Depression.' Cotton was King and it was cotton that built all those beautiful Victorian (gingerbread) homes around the turn of the century. In those days, more cotton was ginned in Ellis County than in any other county in the nation.

Autumn brings back many warm memories of freshly picked cotton in wagons pulled by horses or mules. Saturdays were the really exciting days downtown with grocery shopping, getting hair cut, seeing doctors, visiting lawyers, checking in with your banker and maybe going to one of the three 'picture shows' around the Square. Downtown was full of people and was an exciting place to visit friends, or just 'watch the parade' of so many people gathering together in a spirit of fun and laughter.

During the summer months, we always went barefoot, except on Sunday to go to Church. We enjoyed roaming around town through the Courthouse and up the circular staircase in the tower. Children seemed to take care of their own entertainment in those days with baseball on vacant land where we made our own playing field, and played tin-can-shinny on roller skates in the street using a tin can for the puck and a tree limb for a hockey stick. There were also games such as 'Hide and Seek,' 'Capture the Flag,' 'Red Rover,' or we could ride our bikes or roller skate all over town. We could also pick and enjoy a luscious ripe peach from a neighbor's tree without it being called stealing. On summer days when we were just hanging out in the street and sweltering under the hot sun, the ice wagon, pulled by two mules, would come by and the friendly ice man would throw us a chunk of ice to cool us off. Those were carefree days when children could create their own recreation in a safe environment.

There are many other fond memories. At

Photograph by Kevin Haislip

'Happy's' you could get two delicious hamburgers, potato chips, and a soda for a quarter. You could also go to a café downtown and get the 'Blue Plate Special' for twenty-five cents or the 'Deluxe' for thirty-five cents. A cup of coffee cost a whole nickel.

Many occasions brought friends and families together. Football games in the Fall and men's softball on warm summer evenings. Everyone participated in the parades and picnics on the Fourth of July and Armistice Day. At election time, a stage was built on the South side of the Square and candidates running for election would take their turn to speak and make their pitch to the voters. Then, on election night, a giant blackboard was erected to tabulate the votes. The results were entered on the blackboard. Both of these informative and entertaining political events brought great turnout to the Square as people gathered around the stage to hear the speeches and then later to learn who had won the elections.

There are also great memories of treasured events at Sims Library, Getzendaner Park, and the Chautauqua, all of which add to the charm and beauty of our town. These are just a sampling of my memories. But events before my time and after my time all become a part of the fabric that has been woven into what we like to call 'Historic Waxahachie.'

Although I always kept in touch, college, World War II and a career carried me away from Waxahachie for about fifty years. However, the charm and the friendliness of the town drew me back, and it was great coming home. I was welcomed and given the opportunity to become an active part of our town. This included involvement in Historic Waxahachie, the Symphony Association, Waxahachie Foundation, the Education Foundation, the Ellis County Museum, church, and volunteering as a mentor in the Waxahachie Public Schools. I even had the privilege of being elected to the City Council and then was very honored to become Mayor.

Waxahachie is a warm and friendly town that welcomes and encourages everyone to become part of the community and spirit of Waxahachie.

I love Waxahachie and I know you will too!

Joe Jenkins, Mayor
City of Waxahachie

Joe Jenkins

'Doc' Johnson, Northside Elementary crossing guard. Photograph by Sally Owens

Chautauqua Preservation Society stages its 2006 season with *The Power of Storytelling*. Clockwise from upper left: the Chautauqua Auditorium in Getzendaner Park built in 1902, *Dr. Bluefield's Attoyac Valley Medicine Show*, and Cynthia Dorn Navarrete as the Black Diva Sissieretta Jones in *Black Diva-The Voice of Angels*. All crowd pleasers.

Photographs of the event by Ismael and Shari Alfaro

Photograph by Ami Trull

Neal White covers a story for the Waxahachie Daily Light of the production *Oklahoma* at the Chautauqua Auditorium. Photograph by Kevin Haislip

Ivan and Peggy Cole love to love people. At holiday feasts, they invite friends, family, and new acquaintances to join them for dinner and the celebrations. Photograph by Kevin Haislip

Photograph by Kevin Haislip

Rainbow over Waxahachie's Marvin Elementary. Photograph by Ami Trull

parades & festivals
shopping & dining
antiques & furniture
clothing, specialty & gift shops
museums & galleries

Find yourself downtown,
Picture perfect
year around!

Waxahachie Downtown Merchants Association
and
Waxahachie Chamber of Commerce
and Convention & Visitors Bureau

Santa arrives early each November to open the Enchanted Pines Easy Glide Skate Rink across from City Hall. Photograph by Kevin Haislip

The Festival of Trees, sponsored by The Education Foundation for WISD, opens the season with bright lights and ideas. Trees are donated by individuals and groups, displayed, and auctioned to raise funds for Waxahachie Independent School District teacher grants and student scholarships.
Photograph by Kevin Haislip

Twelve unique homes and homeowners don their holiday finery beginning Thanksgiving for the Candlelight Home Tour. For three weekends, people are invited to see the dazzling and heartwarming displays.
Photograph by Kevin Haislip

Victorian Christmas Celebration on the square brings Jim Jenkins out of his law office to play for shoppers. Photograph by Kevin Haislip

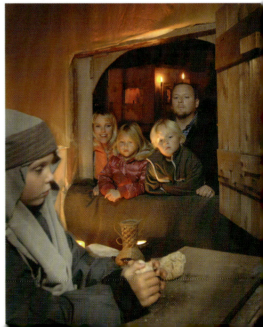

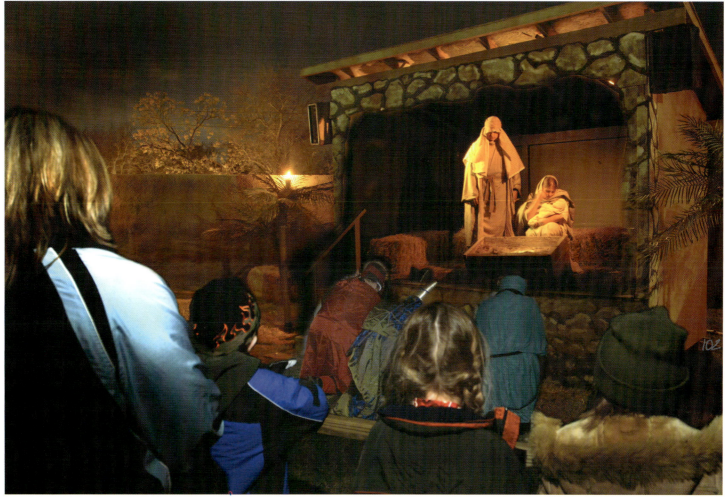

Imagine being able to step back in time 2000 years! Bethlehem Revisited recreates the ancient streets as Mary and Joseph found on the night of Christ's birth. On their journey, they meet innkeepers, merchants, food vendors, craftsmen, tradesmen, clergy, and citizens as well as live sheep, camels, and donkeys.

Bethlehem Revisited is considered one of the top attractions in the state of Texas at Christmas time. The cast of over 175 Waxahachians from nearly every church in the area donned custumes and presented the true meaning of Christmas, the birth of Jesus Christ, to over 30,000 visitors. Photographs by Kevin Haislip

Local Artist Don Locke made a mosaic quilt using tiny squares of fabric to recreate Leonardo da Vinci's Last Supper. Every year, Central Presbyterian Church displays the quilt in the sanctuary during Bethlehem Revisited for visitors to warm themselves and meditate on Jesus' life and His sacrifice for mankind.

Photographs by Kevin Haislip

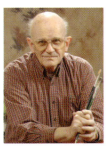

Photograph by Lynn Cromer

104

Photograph by Kevin Haislip

The adoption is finally complete for Kayla and Kody by Steve and Kathryn Bounds. Judge Bob Carroll held the first Adoption Day for Ellis County on December 1, 2006 with plans to make it an annual event. This morning, nine families completed their adoption of 13 children before his bench. At the end of the day, Judge Carroll said it was the best day he had ever had in his courtroom. Photograph by Kevin Haislip

Waxahachie City Council on September 18, 2006 left to right: Councilman Joe Gallo, Councilman Chuck Beatty, Councilman Joe Jenkins, Mayor Jay Barksdale, Councilman Ron Wilkinson.
Photograph by Kevin Haislip

Jerry Seevers ends a long day with cutting his grandson Cole's hair. Photograph by Kevin Haislip

Waxahachie Lake. Photograph by Kevin Haislip

Photograph by Sally Owens

Photograph by Ami Trull

Thirty cars from businesses around Waxahachie race around the streets downtown for the Waxahachie Lion's annual Mini Grand Prix. The event is a fund raiser for the Lions and proceeds have been used for Lion's Club Charities, and to support local civic projects.   Photographs by Gerry Heine

Historic Rogers Street Bridge. Photograph by Ami Trull

Underneath the Elm Street Viaduct.
Photograph by Sally Owens

Midlothian/Waxahachie 'Mid-way Regional Airport' on Highway 287. Photograph by Kevin Haislip

David and Paula Hudgins are building their Train Depot home around a 1926 Pullman car they have been restoring. Photograph by Kevin Haislip

Mike Grant catches a quick burger at Oma's Jiffy Burger, a long time quick stop.   Photograph by Ami Trull.

The Woman's Building was built in 1925, and has been a central meeting place for people since. In the spring of 2007, it received it's historic recognition from the Texas Historic Commission. Photographs by Kevin Haislip

Linda Schindler paints the garden of a home on the Gingerbread Trail Tour of Homes. Ellis County Art Association hosts local artists in the area to paint the homes on display as part of Paint Waxahachie Plain Aire. Photograph by Kevin Haislip

Kenny Kennedy, visiting pastor from Hill County preaches at the Cowboy Church of Ellis County at a Thursday night *Buckout*. The Cowboy Churches got their start in Waxahachie and are affiliated with the Baptist General Convention of Texas. Photograph by Kevin Haislip

Everyone has gone home. Getzendaner Park on a foggy night in winter.   Photography by Kevin Haislip

Family and friends gather to honor Joyce Williams Watson in the Waxahachie Cemetery (born July 23, 1925, died April 5, 2007). Beloved wife of James Raymond Watson (Raymond died January 6, 1998), mother of Rebecca Joyce Watson, William Cullen Watson, Brenda Kathleen Watson Mavridis, and grandmother to six. She was the daughter of Ross and Vera Williams who were cotton and wheat farmers and ranchers in Waxahachie. Joyce was born in Waxahachie, third generation, and lived almost her entire life here caring for her family. She now rests alongside her husband in the town that meant so much to her. Photograph by Kevin Haislip

Epilogue

There are a lot of stories and pictures that make up people's lives in our little corner of the world. Waxahachie is a small town on an ever increasingly small planet in a vast galaxy. At the recent city council meeting, it was announced that our population is now 28,200. The current world population is 6,525,170,264.

We are a people of faith and community. For whatever we do that is right, we thank God. Whatever we do that is wrong, we trust that God makes all things right for those who trust in Him. We do.

Our town has two orphan homes in its boundaries: the Texas Baptist Children's Home, and the Presbyterian Children's Home. Habitat for Humanity and their volunteers work tirelessly to give dignity and homeownership to those struggling just to get by. The many other community organizations that support us in so many ways have volunteers who deliver meals to our seniors, help for pregnant young women without resources, and provide food and financial assistance for the destitute. As Neal White and Wanda Cain wrote, we embrace the strangers who come into our town.

The stories we have failed to print, the pictures we did not get are a reflection of a story way too big to tell in a book.

We have something pretty special here.

The Publisher

Photograph by Kevin Haislip

Dwayne Swindle takes a couple of children fishing on the Waxahachie campus of the Presbyterian Children's Homes and Services.   The Presbyterian Children's Home cares for 60 children on its campus, plus oversees a number in private foster care homes in the community. The Texas Baptist Home for Children cares for 27 children on its campus and another 53 placed in private foster care homes. Photograph by Kevin Haislip

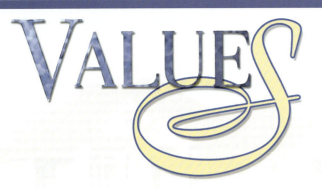

We at Texas Heritage Custom Homes are proud of our reputation of Value and our history of Values.

Lance & Laurie Whitlock
972-923-2400

www.texasheritagecustomhomes.com

The UPS Store™
In Waxahachie!

791 Hwy 77N, Suite 501C
(New Beall's Shopping Center)
Phone: 972-351-9310
FAX: 972-351-9370
store5780@theupsstore.com

©2003 United Parcel Service, Inc.

- Shipping Services
- Packaging Services
- Mailbox & Postal Services
- Copying Services
- Notary Services
- Passport Photos
- Printing Services
- Faxing Services

"Hometown Radio for Waxahachie since 1955"

KBEC
classic country
1390

711 Ferris Avenue
Waxahachie, Texas
(972) 938-1390

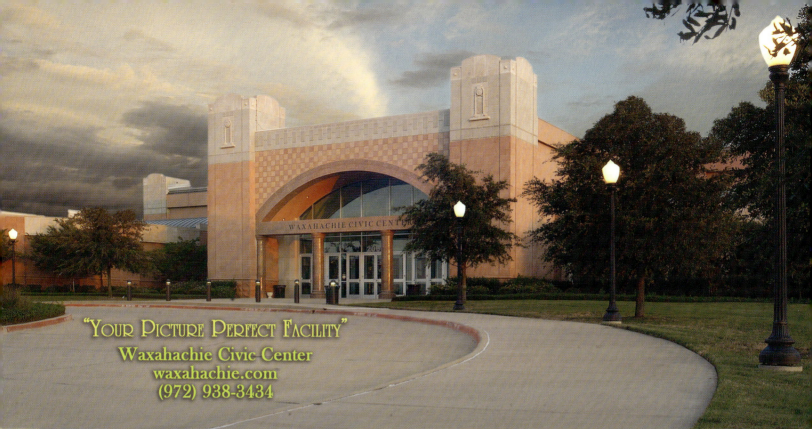

"Your Picture Perfect Facility"
Waxahachie Civic Center
waxahachie.com
(972) 938-3434

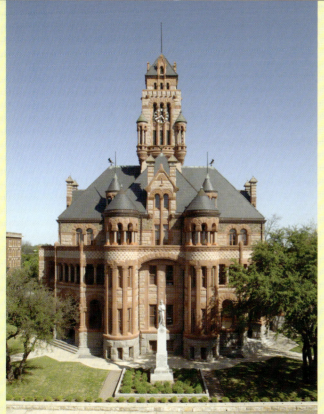

Ellis County Abstract & Title
Closing your family & friends for over 70 years

Waxahachie 972 938-2601
408 Ferris Avenue

Red Oak 972 617-7200
230 East Ovilla Road

Midlothian 972 723-7971
109 North 8th Street